ALL BIRDS HAVE
ANXIETY

KATHY HOOPMANN

Jessica Kingsley *Publishers*
London and Philadelphia

In a perfect world, everyone would cope with life just fine, and no one would be anxious or worried.

But the truth is, we do not live in a perfect world and everyone experiences life in different ways.

Some people feel anxious and worried about anything and everything.

Of course,
everyone feels
anxious sometimes,
which can be good
when you need
to take care,

or there is danger nearby.

Being anxious can also help you hurry when things need to be done.

However, some of us are anxious
even when we are not in danger
and life seems to be going well.

The "take-care" thoughts,
the "danger" warnings, and
the "hurry" urges get out
of control and become
monsters in our minds.

When stress builds up, anything can set off anxiety, such as:

a change of plan,

something new,

a comment,

a thought.

Stuff.

Even *thinking* about being anxious
can make you anxious.

Many people
have anxiety
and it often
runs in families.

First comes an uneasy feeling that grows
and grows until you are so scared that
you can't move or breathe.

Often you don't even know why.

Your mouth goes dry, it's hard to swallow and your stomach hurts.

You may get dizzy and sweaty, and have headaches. Your heart pounds. Hands and feet can tingle or go numb. Every muscle is tense.

It's like being filled with a scream.

Anxiety also affects how we think, feel and act.

We are sure that nothing we ever do, say or try is good enough.

Even if we do well, we are certain it was a mistake.

When we are overwhelmed and frightened, we see everything that goes wrong and nothing that goes right.

Over and over again, we worry
about the future and replay the
daft things we did in the past,
never stopping to enjoy "now."
There is no "off" button.

Our minds become a fog.

We sit and stare with brains like cotton wool and don't know what to do or how to do it.

Everyday jobs,
like combing hair,
changing clothes
or making decisions,
are too much to
think about.

To make things worse,
we don't sleep well.

We lie there, knowing we *have* to sleep.
Then we worry that we *can't* sleep,
which stops us from sleeping. Arghhhh!

Wide-awake thoughts churn in our minds.

All that makes us completely exhausted.

Other times we may panic. "Calm down," people say. "Things aren't that bad!" But they don't understand that when fear grips your brain, it takes over your body and you will do anything to get to safety.

Anxiety can make us hyper-aware of what needs to be done *now.*

It's worse when people say, "Why don't you just start?"

We *know* we need to start but we don't know how!

So days can go by when nothing gets
done and our jobs pile up around us.

Anxiety is much worse when we
can't control what happens.

Therefore, we try to order our lives, and those around us, to avoid surprises.

Some of us do the same things in the same way, which makes us feel safe.

Sadly, we can't
control everything
all the time so we
constantly struggle
to cope when life
changes.

Sometimes friends say, "Let's go for
a walk. It will do you good."

And it *does* make us feel better.

But no one realises how hard
it is to leave the safety of
home if you are aware of every
possible thing that can go wrong.

Even if we want company, the thought
of being in a crowd fills us with fear.

We have no idea what to say,
where to go or how to behave.

We are worried that others will watch
everything we do, and judge us.

Sometimes we are so tense that
we can snap at others.

Often we go off by ourselves, cancel
plans, leave early or just don't turn up.

It's hard for those around us when we act like that, and we are very sorry. We never mean to upset anybody.

I just don't understand!

Other times we can pretend that life is fine and we can have a laugh with friends.

We can't keep that up for long
though, and soon need time to
be alone in a safe place.

If anyone comes looking for us, we hide.

We don't have the energy to chat.
Besides, we know they wish we felt
better and we don't want to let
them down or be a bother.

For a while, it helps to be by ourselves. Then we start to fear that we will be alone forever.

So, it's like this.

What you think affects how you feel.

Then how you feel affects the way you act.

Fearing the worst can make you feel and act as if you are helpless.

But the fact is that you are *not* helpless
and there *are* things you can do to reduce
the power anxiety has over your life.

Starting something new!
Walking out the door!
Dogs! Speaking in public!
Spiders! Planes!
School! Heights!
Changing my routine!
Homework!
A party!

For example, avoiding something
you fear makes it grow **BIGGER** and
SCARIER in your mind.

The amazing thing is when you force yourself to face what scares you, or you start whatever it is you are worried about, the scariness shrinks.

Starting something new! Walking out the door! Speaking in public! Dogs! Planes! Spiders! Heights! School! Changing my routine! Homework! A party!

You don't have to jump in all at once. From a safe place, you can watch how others cope.

Then you can have a little try
with someone you trust,

until slowly, you are brave enough
to face your fears on your own.

Then you will find that the things you thought would be terrible have no real terror in them, and things you thought would be horrible are not full of horror.

It's also good to remember that anxiety is not your fault and it will not rule you forever. Then you can practise choosing to think about things in a different way.

Not doing it will make me more anxious than doing it.
I don't have to be perfect.
It's great I tried my hardest.
The world won't end if I make a mistake.

It can help if you don't fear anxiety when it comes along. Instead, accept it with an annoyed sigh.

oh, it's you again.

Seeing it as something outside of you
gives you power over it.

Exercise, plenty of sunshine and a healthy diet are all a huge help.

So is snuggling a pet.

Being with those who listen to us and accept us makes a world of difference.

Learning how to relax and how to breathe deeply can bring peace.

Caring for others in need can help you
forget your own worries for a while.

Until finally, there will come a time when you can glide through your days without anxiety.

Then you can look forward to
whatever the future brings,

and, even better, you can
be happy living it.

BIRD NAMES AND PHOTOGRAPH CREDITS

Cover image
Snowy owl
© Elenarts

page 1
Macaw parrots
© bluehand

page 2
Duck
© fotofactory

page 3
Great grey owl
© Eric Isselee

page 4
Budgerigar
© nodff

page 5
Unnamed bird
© Mark Wolters

page 6
Weaver bird
© Boonchuay Promjiam

page 7
Brahma hen
© Eric Isselee

page 8
North American bald
eagle
© Stefano Venturi

page 9
Long-eared owl
© aaltair

page 10
Griffon vulture
© MarclSchauer

page 11
Geese
© Vishnevskiy Vasily

page 12
Northern gannet
© Martin Prochazkacz

page 13
Adelle penguin
© Jo Crebbin

page 14
Formosa blue magpie
© PhotonCatcher

page 15
Pelican
© Preobrajenskiy

page 16
Duckling
© Africa Studio

page 17
Young green herons
© Leigh Kennedy

page 18
Roosters
© photomaster

page 19
Crested guinea fowl
© JMx Images

page 20
Puffin
© Martin Oldfield

page 21
Marabou bird, also
known as adjutant stork
© Jacqueline Abromeit

page 22
Common potoo
© Fabio Maffei

page 23
Burrowing owl
© Agustin Esmoris

page 24
Owl
© Antonio Gravante

page 25
Tawny frog mouth
© Janelle Lugge

page 26
Greylag goose
© Dennis Jacobsen

page 27
Common pheasant
© Ondrej Prosicky

page 28
Jackdaw
© roundstripe

page 29
Egret
© Carol Afshar

page 30
Ducklings
© Denis Tabler

page 31
Acorn woodpecker
© Jean-Edouard Rozey

page 32
Hyacinth macaw
© worldswildlifewonders

page 33
Blue-footed booby
© farbled

page 34
Kittiwake with arctic fox
© Pauline Oldfield

page 35
Penguins
© Rashman

page 36
King penguins
© jbutcher

page 37
Bluebirds
© Bonnie Taylor Barry

page 38
Great tit
© Anette Linnea Rasmussen

page 39
Swan
© Dmytro Balkhovitin

page 40
Puffins
© Pauline Oldfield

page 41
Kookaburra
© Michael Koenen

page 42
Flamingo
© Sergey Uryadnikov

page 43
Hyacinth macaw
© Ondrej Prosicky

page 44
Emperor penguins
© vladsilver

page 45
Swan
© Paul Aniszewski

page 46
Secretary bird
© Wollertz

page 47
Parakeet
© Darren415

page 48
Tufted penguin
© Maksimilian

page 49
Flamingo
© Elenarts

page 50
Mute swan
© shaftinaction

page 51
Swan
© Renamarie

page 52
Goldeneye duck
© Vishnevskiy Vasily

page 53
Bearded reedling
© sysasya photography

page 54
Long-eared owl
© taviphoto

page 55
Crowded crane
© Wolkenengel565

page 56
Vulture/yellow canary
© Miceking/Eric Isselee

page 57
Love bird
© Eric Isselee

page 58
Sun conure parrot
© PCHT

page 59
Chicken and German shepherd puppy
© Valentina Razumova

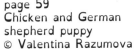
page 60
Barn owls
© GMH Photography

page 61
Lekking black grouse
© Sergey Uryadnikov

page 62
Young impala ram with red-billed oxpecker
© Villiers Steyn

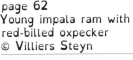
page 63
Kittiwake
© Martin Oldfield

page 64
Chickens
© Andrea Izzotti

page 65
Duckling
© sevenke

First published in 2017
by Jessica Kingsley Publishers
73 Collier Street
London N1 9BE, UK
and
400 Market Street, Suite 400
Philadelphia, PA 19106, USA

www.jkp.com

Library of Congress Cataloging in Publication Data
A CIP catalog record for this book is available from the Library of Congress

British Library Cataloguing in Publication Data
A CIP catalogue record for this book is available from the British Library

ISBN 978 1 78592 182 7
eISBN 978 1 78450 454 0

Printed and bound in China